Microsoft Outlook

Bible

Microsoft Outlook

Bible

By

Jason Taylor

TABLE OF CONTENTS

INTRODUCTION

IMPROVE THE SUBSTANCE OF THE MESSAGE

Not all messages created and sent using Microsoft Outlook must be in plain text. They can have pictures and diagrams, and they can be made more visually appealing by carefully choosing backgrounds, fonts, and colors. You can include a signature with your contact details and possibly your company's logo for more official communications. To draw the recipient's or your attention, you can include visual information in a message, contact list, or other Outlook item.

You could say, for instance, that a communication is very important or that it contains sensitive information. Options that alert you when a recipient receives a message or that stop the receiver from printing or forwarding a message can also be specified.

Creating and using automatic signatures, adding graphics to messages, customizing the formatting of default messages, applying theme elements to specific messages, and modifying message settings and delivery options.

CHAPTER ONE

This chapter includes the following:

- Customize the default message formatting.
- Apply thematic elements to specific messages.
- Create and use automatic signatures.
- Include photos in messages.
- Modify message delivery choices and settings

CUSTOMIZE THE STANDARD MESSAGE FORMAT

An Outlook message's text content is shown by default in black, 11-point Calibri font, which was selected for its readability, with paragraphs aligned to the left on a white background. Similar to working in a Microsoft Word document or Microsoft PowerPoint presentation, you can alter the look of the text in a message by applying either local formatting (character or paragraph attributes and styles that you apply directly to text) or global formatting (a theme or style set that you apply to the entire document). You can remember your settings, though, so Outlook will apply them to both new messages and message responses if you would rather use a particular font and color for every message you write.

The Signatures And Stationery dialog box's Personal Stationery tab is where you configure your default font and theme settings. New messages and responses (forwards and

Signatures and Stationery

E-mail Signature | Personal Stationery

Theme or stationery for new HTML e-mail message

Theme... | No theme currently selected

Font: | Use theme's font

New mail messages:

Font... | Sample Text

Replying or forwarding messages:

Font... | Sample Text

☐ Mark my comments with: Samantha Smith
☐ Pick a new color when replying or forwarding

Composing and reading plain text messages:

Font... | Sample Text

OK | Cancel

replies) have different font formatting settings. (You must select the same font twice, even if you wish to utilize it.)

Calibri is set to blue for responses and black for original texts by default. To visually distinguish between your responses and the original message content within a message trail, you might keep using various colors. Alternatively, you may want to use the same font for all of your messages, whether or not they are new. This will make it easier for receivers to identify the content of your messages. You can choose from every option in the Font dialog box while you're establishing default fonts. You can choose from the entire selection of fonts for emails.

Squares in the font effect check boxes show that the effects are not on or off, which is essentially the same as being off. You have the option to leave these alone or to explicitly activate an effect.

Selecting a font face that is easy to read is the best option. Some things to think about are:

- Character width
- Both capital and lowercase letters

Character width: Wide typefaces might take up a lot of room, while narrow fonts can be difficult to read.

Both capital and lowercase letters: Certain fonts only show capital letters. The numbers are easily readable. For instance, the lowercase letter "o" and the numeral zero are displayed nearly identically in some fonts. Sending someone a password that contains a zero could be challenging for them to read if you set one of these as your default font.

The words Sample Text in the font you choose are shown in the Preview section of the Font dialog box. That doesn't cover everything, so before choosing, you might want to test out a few typefaces in an email message.

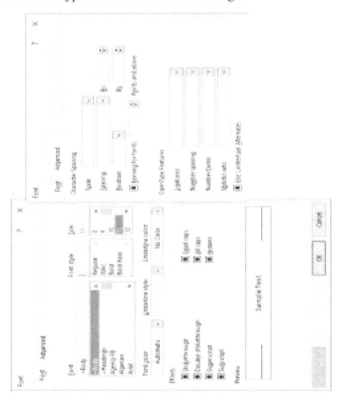

The Body font is the default message font that you set in the Font dialog box. Unlike when producing documents in Word or worksheets in Excel, there are no fonts to set besides the message font, hence the "Set As" Default button does not become active. Outlook information fields, including those in message headers, contact data, and appointments, cannot have their font changed.

Another font option from this dialog box affects how plain-text communications you receive seem in Outlook when you view them. Many individuals use their cellphones to send emails, and they can set up their messages to be transmitted in plain text or HTML. (You can also select one of these message kinds for subscription-based messages, like reminders about package deliveries.) It is easier for software to render and display plain text messages consistently. Calibri will display plain text messages until you choose a different default.

You can designate an email message theme, which is a pre-selected collection of fonts, colors, and graphic components that Outlook will use when you create messages, in addition to the message typefaces. By checking or unchecking the Background Image check box, you can add or remove the colored or illustrated graphic background that comes with most themes.

Fonts, colors, page backgrounds, and inline graphic components are examples of email message themes. Selecting stationery (think of this as selecting patterned paper on which to write letters) is an alternative to selecting a full theme. While some stationery alternatives are more subdued (green bubbles on a green background), others feature really striking graphic images (dozens of teddy bears parading over the page). While the graphics in some stationery options fill the entire page, others limit them to the left border of the email "page" to provide room for text and other email content. Options for stationery range from understated to colorful.

As was previously covered in this topic, you must define your default message font independently from the stationery you choose. Choose a font color that will stand out against the stationery backdrop and be readable by recipients who have chosen to block graphic components in emails if you decide to use stationery (though I would advise you to use it sparingly). For instance, using crisp white lettering against the brown Jungle stationery background may be alluring, but recipients who block graphics will see white lettering on a white background, making the message appear blank unless they choose to view the content.

TO BRING UP THE DIALOG WINDOW FOR SIGNATURES AND STATIONERY

- To access the Backstage view, select the File tab. To open the Outlook Options dialog box, select Options in the left pane.
- Select the Mail tab in the Outlook Options dialog box's left pane.

Complete one of the following actions in the Compose messages area of the Mail page:

- Click the Signatures button to bring up the E-mail Signature tab.
- Click the Stationery and Fonts button to bring up the Personal Stationery tab.

TO MODIFY THE OUTGOING MESSAGES' DEFAULT FONT

- Open the Signatures and Stationery dialog box and select the Personal Stationery tab.

To open the Font dialog box, do one of the following actions:

- Click the Font button in the New mail messages area to customize the font for new messages.
- In the Replying or forwarding section, click the Font button to customize the font for message responses.
- Choose the font you want Outlook to use for the chosen message type in the Font dialog box. Click OK after that.

TO ALTER THE PLAIN-TEXT MESSAGE DISPLAY'S DEFAULT FONT

- Open the Signatures and Stationery dialog box and select the Personal Stationery tab.
- Click the Font button under the Composing and Reading Plain Text Messages section.
- Choose the typeface you want Outlook to use for plain-text message display in the typeface dialog box. Click OK after that.

TO BRING UP THE STATIONERY OR THEME DIALOG BOX

- Click the Theme button in the Theme or Stationery for new HTML e-mail message section of the Signatures and Stationery dialog box's Personal Stationery tab.

TO DESIGNATE A THEME FOR
COMMUNICATIONS THAT ARE SENT

- Launch the Stationery or Theme dialog box.

- To get a preview in the right pane, click on any entry in the Choose a Theme pane that doesn't finish in (Stationery).

- Choose or clear any of the following check boxes to view the theme options that have been modified: Bright hues, lively graphics, and a background image

- Click OK once you have chosen and configured the desired theme.

Follow these steps if you wish to use a font other than the theme font:

- Click the Font list to bring up the options in the Signatures and Stationery dialog box's Theme or Stationery for new HTML e-mail message section.

Choose one of the actions listed in the Font list:

E-mail Signature	Personal Stationery		
Theme or stationery for new HTML e-mail message			
Theme...	Blue Calm		
Font:	Use theme's font		
New mail	Use theme's font		
	Use my font when replying and forwarding messages		
	Always use my fonts		

- Click Use my font when replying and forwarding messages to create original messages using the theme

17

font, but use the font specified in the Replying Or Forwarding Messages section for responses.

- Click Always use my fonts to utilize the other theme elements instead of the theme font.

TO DESIGNATE BACKDROP STATIONERY FOR MESSAGES THAT ARE SENT

- Launch the Stationery or Theme dialog box.

- To get a preview in the right pane, click on any entry in the Choose a Theme pane that has (Stationery) added to the name.

- Click OK once you've chosen the backdrop stationery you want.

Include thematic components in each message. With just a few clicks, you can apply global formatting options—by employing themes and style sets—if you would rather apply thematic aspects to specific messages.

CHAPTER TWO

USE AND SWITCH UP THE THEMES

The Themes gallery on the Options tab in a message composition window offers nine of the standard Microsoft Office themes (not the same as the email message themes you can choose in the Theme Or Stationery dialog box). The message's usage of color, typeface, and graphic effects is determined by each theme.

The Office theme is used by default in all Word documents, PowerPoint presentations, Microsoft Excel workbooks, email messages, and other Office products. The Office theme controls the colors, fonts, and effects in your message if you don't apply another theme.

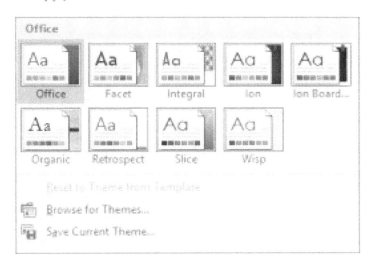

By altering the color scheme, font selection, or effect style, you can change the formatting that the current theme applies.

To alter a message's theme, first select the theme you wish to use by clicking the Themes button in the Themes group on the Options tab of the message composing window.

To alter a message's color scheme, take one of the following actions:

- Select the color scheme you wish to use by clicking the Colors button (the ScreenTip indicates Theme Colors) in the Themes group on the Options tab of the message composing window.
- Click the Change Styles button in the Styles group on the Format Text tab of the message composing window. Then, click Colors and select the color scheme you wish to use.

To modify the font set used in a message, do one of the following:

- Click the Fonts button (the ScreenTip indicates Theme Fonts) in the Themes group on the Options tab of the message composing window, and then select the font set you wish to use.

- Select the font set you wish to use by clicking the Change Styles button in the Styles group on the Format Text tab of the message composing window.

To modify the effect style applied in a message, click the Effects button (the ScreenTip indicates Theme Effects) in the Themes group of the Options tab of the message composing window. Next, click the effect you wish to apply.

CHANGE AND APPLY STYLES

Email messages can be formatted using styles just like Word documents, but most people won't write emails with the same length and level of information that would necessitate those, so we'll only touch on them in passing in this book. Character and paragraph styles can be applied from the separate Styles pane or from the Format Text tab's Styles gallery. The Styles pane has the advantage of remaining accessible and open while you work. The pane can be left floating anywhere on the screen or docked to the window's right side.

The styles you wish to see in the Styles Gallery and Styles pane can be specified. Individual styles' typefaces, colors, and paragraph formatting are all altered by a style set. You can choose from any of the 17 available style sets (or make your own) to alter the look of every style in a message. The icons in the Styles gallery and all of the text in the current message change appearance when a style set is selected.

- Click the More button in the Styles group on the Format Text tab to enlarge the Styles gallery in its entirety.
- Click the Styles dialog box launcher on the Format Text tab to access the Styles pane.

The Styles pane can be moved

- Point to the header of the Styles pane.
- Drag the pane when the pointer turns into a four-headed arrow.

Take any of these actions:

- You can move the pane to any part of the screen.

To dock the pane to the message composition window, drag it to the inside edge of the window. To undock it, drag it away from the docking spot.

To use a style

- To format a word or paragraph, click anywhere within it, or choose the text you wish to format.
- Select the style you wish to use from the Styles window or gallery.

To alter a message's style set

- Click the Change Styles button in the Styles category on the Format Text tab.
- Select the desired style set by clicking Style Set on the Change Styles menu.

MAKE AND UTILIZE AUTOMATED SIGNATURES

You will almost certainly "sign" an email message by adding your name at the end of the message text when you send it to someone. By generating an email signature and linking it to your email account, Outlook may automatically include your signature text in outgoing messages. You can add extra information to your email signature that you would like message recipients to know every time.

Formatted text and images can be included in an email signature. In addition to your name and contact details, a standard email signature may also contain your company name, job title, legal disclaimer, corporate or personal motto, photo, and other details, depending on the circumstances. Your electronic business card might even be a part of your email signature. You can make distinct signatures to use in various message formats or when sending messages from several email accounts. For example, you could make a personal signature for messages sent from another account, a casual business signature for interoffice correspondence, and a formal business signature for client correspondence. You could also make a signature with less information to send with message replies and one with more information to send with original email messages. Similar to how you format message content, you can format the text of your email signature. You can create and format your signature in an email message composition window, copy it, and then paste it into the signature content pane if you wish to apply formatting that isn't accessible through the buttons at the top of the pane.

If you want to do something more elaborate, make the signature look you want in an email message composition window, save a screen capture of it as a graphic, and then insert the graphic into the signature content box. A signature can have inline images, but the signature content pane does not support wrapping text around images.

You can either apply a different email signature to each account or the same email signature to all of the accounts if Outlook is set up to connect to multiple email accounts. When you send new messages from a particular account, the signature you designate for that account will be automatically displayed. Any email signature you've made can also be manually added to any message. Outlook replaces any current email signature by inserting the new one at the end of the message.

TO BRING UP THE SIGNATURES AND STATIONERY DIALOG BOX'S E-MAIL SIGNATURE TAB

- Open the Outlook Options dialog box and bring up the Mail page from any module.
- Click the Signatures button in the Compose messages section.

Or

- Select the Insert or Message tab in a message composing window.
- Click the Signature icon in the Include group, and then select Signatures.

TO MAKE A BASIC SIGNATURE

- Open the Signatures and Stationery dialog box and select the E-mail Signature tab. The Select Signature To Edit box displays a list of all current signatures.
- Click the New button beneath the Select signature to edit box. Before you can interact with the signature material, Outlook asks you to provide a name for the new signature.

- Choose a name that will help you distinguish this signature from others you generate, such Work or Disclaimer, in the Type a name for this signature box. After that, click OK to generate the signature and make it editable.

- Type the words you wish to include in the Edit signature box. If you'd like, format the font. Your signature's formatted components will show up in emails precisely like they do here.
- Click Save once the basic signature is complete.

TO MODIFY AN ALREADY-EXISTING EMAIL SIGNATURE

- Open the Signatures and Stationery dialog box and select the E-mail Signature tab.
- Click the signature you wish to modify in the Select signature to edit box to bring it up in the Edit Signature pane.
- Click the Save button after making any necessary adjustments.

TO INCLUDE A PICTURE INLINE INTO AN EMAIL SIGNATURE

- Open the Signatures and Stationery dialog box and select the E-mail Signature tab.
- Choose an existing signature to modify or create a new one.
- Click to place the pointer where you wish to add the image in the Edit signature pane.

- Select the Insert Picture button (the second button from the right) from the toolbar above the pane.

- Click Insert after choosing and browsing to the image you wish to insert in the Insert Picture dialog box. An inline graphic can be placed anywhere in the text.

- Click the Save button after making any other adjustments.

TO ADORN AN EMAIL SIGNATURE WITH ELEGANT PICTURES

- Create the desired signature in an image editing program, Word document, PowerPoint slide, or email composition window, then save it as an image file. Remove any blank space from the image's edges.

- Open the Signatures and Stationery dialog box and select the E-mail Signature tab.

- Either select an existing signature to modify or create a new one.

- Choose and remove any current content from the image that you do not wish to include in the Edit signature pane.

- To place the cursor where you wish to add the image, click.

- Select the Insert Picture button (the second button from the right) from the toolbar above the pane.
- Choose the image you wish to insert by browsing to it in the Insert Picture dialog box, then click Insert. If you'd like, you can add text to the image as well.
- Click the Save button after making any other adjustments.

TO AUTOMATICALLY INCLUDE A SIGNATURE IN EMAILS SENT

- Open the Signatures and Stationery dialog box and select the E-mail Signature tab.
- Complete the following actions in the "Select default signature" section: Click the account you wish to assign the signature to in the list of email accounts.
- Click the signature you want Outlook to add to all new emails you send from the chosen account in the New Messages list.
- Click the signature you want Outlook to add to all response messages you send from the chosen account in the Replies/Forwards list.
- Click OK in the Signatures and Stationery dialog box.

- To confirm that the signature shows up, compose a fresh email message.

TO MANUALLY ADD AN ALREADY-EXISTING EMAIL SIGNATURE TO A COMMUNICATION

- Select the Insert or Message tab in a message composing window.
- Click the Signature button in the Include group.
- Select the name of the email signature you wish to add from the Signature list.

Just like you would with any other message content, select and remove the email signature material from the message.

Include pictures in your messages. As they say, "a picture is worth a thousand words," and email is a way to share information with others. You can provide visual information in Outlook in the following ways: You can share photos with others by embedding them in messages or attaching them to messages.

By taking screenshots of your screen straight from Outlook and then including them in your message, you may share information from papers, websites, and other visual presentations.

- Use SmartArt visuals to explain complex procedures and other business information in messages or by embedding your own SmartArt graphics in other Office applications.
- Create a chart inside a message to convey statistical data.

All of these kinds of graphics can be added to the notes pane of a contact record or to the content pane of an email, calendar item, or task using the Illustrations group on the Insert tab. (There is one exception: images cannot be included in notes.) Images in an email message are used twice. When you need to effectively communicate facts or concepts in business communications, especially to a worldwide audience, images can be really helpful. You can use SmartArt graphics in Outlook (and other Office programs) to illustrate processes, cycles, hierarchies, and other linkages, and you may use charts to illustrate graphical representations of numerical data.

Lists of information can be represented graphically with SmartArt visuals. By choosing the desired graphic type and then filling it in with the necessary data, you may generate a SmartArt graphic right within an email message. You can structure the SmartArt image with properly themed color schemes and effects, alter the graphic type if your first choice doesn't best convey the final information, and alter the image to fit the information you wish to convey. Outlook turns the SmartArt image into a static image when you send the message.

Data tables are represented graphically via charts. Excel is commonly used to produce tables and charts. Another option is to make a chart right within an Outlook email. Because they are based on an Excel data source that is generated from within Outlook, charts created in an email message look just like those prepared in an Excel workbook.

A chart or SmartArt graphic that is included in a message that you send or receive is transformed into a static image (a picture) and resized to suit the message window. You will discover that the graphic in the sent message is the same whether you access it from your Sent Items folder. The image can no longer be edited, but it can be copied and used again in other files, including presentations, documents, and mails.

Just like in a Word document or on a PowerPoint slide, you can interact with all of these kinds of photos in an Outlook message. We won't go into great detail on images and graphics in this book because Outlook is mostly about calendaring, email, and contact management.

Modify the delivery options and message parameters. Visual cues about the importance, sensitivity, or subject category of a message or other Outlook item can be included when you send it. You can also flag a message for follow-up, prevent others from altering or forwarding the message content, provide a straightforward feedback mechanism in the form of voting buttons, and customize message delivery options to suit your needs. Some of these choices allow recipients to see icons in the message header right in the Outlook message list.

This message contains a follow-up flag, a status, and a reminder. Sensitivity and voting buttons do not show message header icons. Many of the options in the message viewing window are not represented by icons, but rather by text. Recipients can be informed of requests within the message text by using the Action Items add-in.

The following are typical message settings and delivery choices:

- Reminders and flag: You can add an informative reminder, put an outgoing message on your to-do list, or schedule a reminder to show up for both you and the receivers of the message at a specific time and date. For your information, call, do not forward, follow up, forward, no response necessary, and Read, Respond, Respond to Everyone, and Evaluate. The significance By setting a message's significance to High or Low (Normal is the default), you can indicate how urgent it is.

An importance icon displays in the Inbox or other message folder, and a similar banner appears in the message header if the Importance field is part of the view. Sensitivity A message's sensitivity can be adjusted to Confidential, Personal, or secret to indicate that it should be kept secret. A banner indicating a sensitivity level other than Normal displays in the message header, but no indicator is shown in the message folder.

- Safety and security: You can either encrypt the message's contents or digitally sign it if you have a digital ID.
- Options for voting: You can include voting buttons in your messages so that recipients can swiftly choose from multiple-choice response options if both you and the recipients have Microsoft Exchange Server accounts.
- Options for tracking: Requesting delivery and read receipts will allow you to keep track of messages.

When the email is delivered to the recipient and opened by the recipient, the recipient's email server automatically creates these receipts. Requesting receipts does not ensure that they will be delivered; recipients may be asked to consent to their delivery.

- Options for delivery: You can define sophisticated attachment format and encoding options, designate a date and time for the message to be delivered and to expire, and have reply messages sent to an email address other than your own.

The Tags group on the Message tab, the Tracking and More Options groups on the Options tab, and the message composing window itself all offer the most often used options.

The ribbon provides a few messaging alternatives. You can set all the options except follow-up flags in the Properties dialog box by clicking the dialog box launcher located in the lower-right corner of any of these groups. You may manage voting, tracking, delivery, security, and message settings from the Properties dialog box. By limiting the message permissions, you can limit what other people can do with the communications they receive from you. You can, for instance, stop recipients from copying the message's text, forwarding or printing it, or altering it when they respond to it. (Message attachments are also subject to restrictions.) Permission options can be found in the Permission group on the Options tab and on the Info page of the Backstage view within a message window.

TO BRING UP THE PROPERTIES DIALOG BOX

Select the dialog box launcher from any of the following groups on the ribbon of the message creation window:

- The Message tab's Tags group
- The Options tab's Tracking group
- The Options tab's More Options group

CHAPTER THREE
TO CONVEY THE SIGNIFICANCE OF A MESSAGE

Take one of the actions listed below: Click High Importance or Low Importance in the Tags group on the Message tab to bring up the Properties dialog box. Select Low, Normal, or High from the Importance list in the Settings section.

To show how sensitive a statement is:

- The Properties dialog box will open.
- Click Normal, Personal, Private, or Confidential in the Sensitivity list under the Settings section.

TO INCLUDE COMMON VOTING BUTTONS IN A MESSAGE

Take one of the actions listed below:

- To view the Use Voting Buttons list, select Use Voting Buttons under the Tracking group on the Options tab.
- Launch the Properties dialog box. Click the "Use voting buttons" check box in the Voting and Tracking settings section. Next, make the adjacent list larger.
- Select one of the following options from the list: Accept/Reject, Yes, No, Maybe, Yes, No

- If you opened the Properties dialog box in step 1,

close it now.

- Voting buttons have been added to the outgoing message, as confirmed by an information bar at the top of the message.

TAKE ONE OF THE ACTIONS LISTED BELOW:

- Choose Use Voting Buttons in the Tracking category on the Options page, and then choose Custom. The Properties dialog box will open. Click the "Use voting buttons" check box in the Voting and Tracking settings section.

- Choose and remove any existing button labels from the Use voting buttons box. Next, add your desired custom button labels, separating them with semicolons.

- Close the dialog box for properties.

TO REQUEST RECEIPTS FOR MESSAGES

- Choose one or both of the following check boxes in the Voting and Tracking options section of the Properties dialog box or in the Tracking group on the Options tab: For this mail, request a delivery receipt. For this message, request a read receipt.

- If you opened the Properties dialog box in step 1, close it now.

TO ROUTE RESPONSE MESSAGES TO AN ALTERNATE EMAIL ADDRESS

Take one of the following actions:

- Click "Direct Replies To" in the More Options group on the Options tab. The Properties dialog box will open. Click the "Have replies sent to" check box in the Delivery choices section.

- Choose and remove the current recipient from the Have replies sent to box. Next, type the email address or addresses you would like responses to be sent to, separated by semicolons.

- Close the dialog box for properties.

TO POSTPONE A MESSAGE'S DELIVERY

Choose one of the following actions:

- Click Delay Delivery in the More Options category on the Options tab.

- The Properties dialog box will open. Choose the "Do not deliver before" check box in the Delivery choices section.

- Choose or input the day and time you wish to postpone delivery till, located to the right of "Do not deliver before."

- Close the dialog box for properties.

TO SPECIFY A MESSAGE'S EXPIRATION DATE

The Properties dialog box will open.

- Click the Expires after check box in the Delivery choices section.

- Choose or type the time and date you would like the message to expire in the box to the right of "Expires after."

- Shut down the Properties dialogue window. Both the message header and the message list notify the recipient when a message expires.

Both the sender and the recipient have their mails marked as expired.

TO MARK A MESSAGE SO THE RECIPIENT CAN FOLLOW UP

- Click Follow Up in the Tags category on the Message pane, and then click Add Reminder. The Custom dialog box appears.

- Choose the Flag for Recipients check box in the Custom dialog box after clearing the Flag for Me check box.

- Complete the following actions in the Flag for Recipients section:

- Click Follow up (or any other available flag) in the Flag to list.
- Choose the Reminder check box and then enter the date and time of the reminder if you would like it to be shown to the recipient.

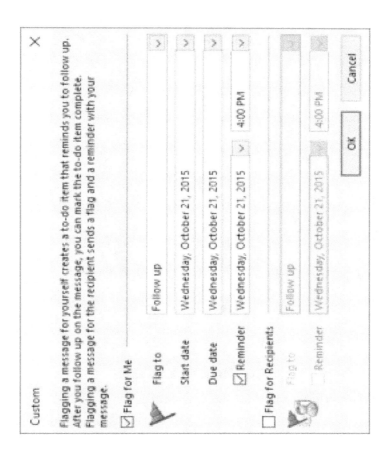

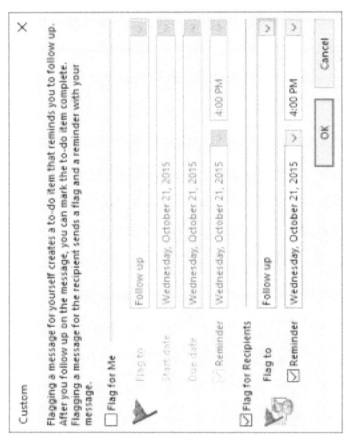

- Click OK in the Custom dialog box.

PRACTICE EXERCISES

Customize the standard message format.

Launch Outlook, and then finish these tasks:

- Open the Signatures and Stationery dialog box and select the Personal Stationery tab.
- Choose the typeface, font size, and font color you wish to use as the default for new messages and responses.
- Launch the Stationery or Theme dialog box.
- Examine the stationery pages and themes that are offered. Think about what would happen if you used one of them in your regular letters.
- Click OK to apply the change after selecting a theme or stationery background that you think will improve your messages. If not, select Cancel.
- Go over the font selections and pick the one you wish to use if you selected a theme in step 3. After that, exit the dialog box.

Show your inbox and test your settings by doing the following:

- Write some text in a new email message.
- Type some text in response to an email you received.
- Close the unsent messages, repeat this series of steps, and adjust the settings if you're unhappy with the outcomes of your choices.

- If requested, remove the message drafts and close the unsent messages after you're satisfied with the outcome.

Include thematic components in each message. After displaying your inbox, finish the following tasks:

- Start a fresh email correspondence.
- Open the ApplyThemes document in Word from the practice file folder, then select Print Layout view.
- Choose the text that begins Office Procedures and continues through the website URL in the ApplyThemes document. The text is then copied to the clipboard.
- Paste the copied content into the message content pane in the message composition window you previously opened. Observe how the formatting of the text instantly changes.
- Modify the message composition window's size to ensure that all of the content is visible. Next, show the window's Options tab.
- Show the Colors menu in the Themes group. (Make sure the menu is open and you can still read the message heads.) To see a real-time preview of how various color schemes affect the message content,

point to them. Next, select a color scheme that appeals to you. Take note of the altered formatting in the message.

- Show the Fonts menu in the Themes group. Click on a font set you like after pointing to various font sets to see them in the message. Take note of how the message's substance has changed.

- Show the message creation window's Format Text tab.

- Open the Style Set gallery from the Styles group. Click on a style set you like after pointing to other style sets to see how they affect the message. Take note of how the message's substance has changed.

- If you would like, send a message to yourself after entering the SBS style test in the Subject field. Otherwise, don't save or send the message; instead, exit the message creation window.

CHAPTER FOUR

MAKE AND UTILIZE AUTOMATED SIGNATURES

After displaying your inbox, finish the following tasks:

- Open the Signatures and Stationery dialog box and select the E-mail Signature tab.

- Make sure your primary email account has a suitable email signature. A company slogan, a favorite quote, contact details, or other text could be included, or it could just be your name. Give the email signature a suitable name.

- Use the email account you made the signature for to apply it to new messages if Outlook doesn't do it automatically.

- To view your inbox, close the dialog window.

- From your primary account, create a new email message and confirm that the signature is included.

- Replay the E-mail Signature tab in the Signatures and Stationery dialog box from the message composition window.

- Choose the signature you made in step 2 and edit it as you see fit. For instance, you may like to include a picture, add formatting, add information, or insert beautiful text from a Word document.

- Go back to the message composing window you started in step 5 after closing the dialog box.
- Manually add the modified email signature after removing the old one from the message.
- Close the window containing the message without transmitting or saving it.
- This is the opportunity to generate other signatures or apply the one you made in step 2 to answers or other accounts.

Include pictures in your messages. Modify the delivery options and message parameters. After displaying your inbox, finish the following tasks:

- Start a fresh email.
- Type your personal email address in the To field. Enter your preference for lunch in the Subject box.
- Type what you would like to have for lunch in the message content pane.
- Perform the following actions using any of the methods outlined in this chapter: Set the importance of the message to low. Decide on Confidential as the sensitivity setting. Include personalized voting buttons in the message that let you select between sandwiches, salad, or pizza.

- Ask for a read receipt as well as a delivery receipt.
- The message should expire in approximately one hour. Set a reminder for a time that is approximately 30 minutes away and flag the message for the recipient to follow up on.
- After sending the message, take these actions: Keep an eye out for the receipts of messages. Once you receive the notification, select your preferred lunch.
- Dismiss the reminder when it arrives.
- Observe how the message window and message list alter once the message expires.

PRACTICE EXERCISES

Customize the standard message format. Launch Outlook, and then finish these tasks:

- Open the Signatures and Stationery dialog box and select the Personal Stationery tab.
- Choose the typeface, font size, and font color you wish to use as the default for new messages and responses.
- Launch the Stationery or Theme dialog box. Examine the stationery pages and themes that are offered. Think about what would happen if you used

one of them in your regular letters. Click OK to apply the change after selecting a theme or stationery background that you think will improve your messages. If not, select Cancel.

- Go over the font selections and pick the one you wish to use if you selected a theme in step 3. After that, exit the dialog box.

Show your inbox and test your settings by doing the following:

- Write some text in a new email message.
- Type some text in response to an email you received.
- Close the unsent messages, repeat this series of steps, and adjust the settings if you're unhappy with the outcomes of your choices.

If requested, remove the message drafts and close the unsent messages after you're satisfied with the outcome. Include thematic components in each message.

After displaying your inbox, finish the following tasks:

- Start a fresh email correspondence.
- Open the ApplyThemes document in Word from the practice file folder, then select Print Layout view.

- Choose the text that begins Office Procedures and continues through the website URL in the ApplyThemes document. The text is then copied to the clipboard.

- Paste the copied content into the message content pane in the message composition window you previously opened. Observe how the formatting of the text instantly changes.

- Modify the message composition window's size to ensure that all of the content is visible. Next, show the window's Options tab.

- Show the Colors menu in the Themes group. (Make sure the menu is open and you can still read the message heads.) To see a real-time preview of how various color schemes affect the message content, point to them. Next, select a color scheme that appeals to you. Take note of the altered formatting in the message.

- Show the Fonts menu in the Themes group. Click on a font set you like after pointing to various font sets to see them in the message. Take note of how the message's substance has changed.

- Show the message creation window's Format Text tab.

- Open the Style Set gallery from the Styles group. Click on a style set you like after pointing to other style sets to see how they affect the message. Take note of how the message's substance has changed.

- If you would like, send a message to yourself after entering the SBS style test in the Subject field. Otherwise, don't save or send the message; instead, exit the message creation window.

MAKE AND UTILIZE AUTOMATED SIGNATURES

After displaying your inbox, finish the following tasks:

- Open the Signatures and Stationery dialog box and select the E-mail Signature tab.

- Make sure your primary email account has a suitable email signature. A company slogan, a favorite quote, contact details, or other text could be included, or it could just be your name. Give the email signature a suitable name.

- Use the email account you made the signature for to apply it to new messages if Outlook doesn't do it automatically.

- To view your inbox, close the dialog window.

- From your primary account, create a new email message and confirm that the signature is included.

- Replay the E-mail Signature tab in the Signatures and Stationery dialog box from the message composition window.

- Choose the signature you made and edit it as you see fit. For instance, you may like to include a picture, add formatting, add information, or insert beautiful text from a Word document.

- Go back to the message composing window you started after closing the dialog box.

- Manually add the modified email signature after removing the old one from the message.

- Close the window containing the message without transmitting or saving it.

- This is the opportunity to generate other signatures or apply the one you made to answers or other accounts.

Include pictures in your messages.

Modify the delivery options and message parameters. After displaying your inbox, finish the following tasks:

- Start a fresh email message.

- Type your personal email address in the To field. Enter your preference for lunch in the Subject box.

- Type what you would like to have for lunch in the message content pane.

Perform the following actions using any of the methods outlined in this chapter:

- Set the importance of the message to low. Decide on Confidential as the sensitivity setting.
- Include personalized voting buttons in the message that let you select between sandwiches, salad, or pizza.
- Ask for a read receipt as well as a delivery receipt.
- The message should expire in approximately one hour.
- Set a reminder for a time that is approximately 30 minutes away and flag the message for the recipient to follow up on.

After sending the message, take these actions:

- Keep an eye out for the receipts of messages.
- Once you receive the notification, select your preferred lunch.
- Dismiss the reminder when it arrives.
- Observe how the message window and message list alter once the message expires.

The Info-Bar at the top of the window shows that the

appointment is next to another on your calendar if you make one that comes right after or before another. The InfoBar notifies you when one appointment clashes with another if you create one that overlaps in time with an already-existing appointment.

You only need to supply the date in order to organize an event. An event can be scheduled immediately on the calendar or during an appointment slot.

Events appear on the calendar in the date section and appointments appear in the time slots when the Calendar view is selected.

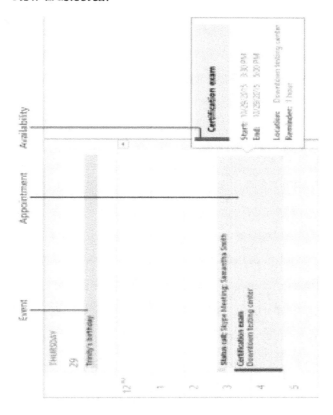

To start a new window for appointments, perform one of the following actions in the Calendar module:

- Click New Appointment under the New group on the Home tab.

Hit Ctrl+N. or Do one of the following in any module:

- Click New Items in the New group on the Home tab, and then click Appointment.
- Hit Ctrl+Shift+A.

TO MAKE AN APPOINTMENT

- Launch a fresh window for appointments.
- Type the appointment's identifying name in the Subject field.
- If applicable, add the appointment location in the Location box. You can also include any other information you would like to have in the appointment heading.
- Enter or choose a date and time in the Start time row. A half hour after the start time, Outlook automatically sets the End Time.
- Enter or choose a date and time in the End time row. An appointment may take place across several days or even overnight.

- Click the Save & Close button in the Actions group on the Appointment pane.

Or

Show the calendar in the Calendar view's Day, Work Week, or Week arrangement. In the calendar pane, perform one of the following actions:

- On the day of the appointment, click the time slot at the appointment start time.
- Drag from the beginning of the appointment until the finish of it.
- Make basic appointments straight from the calendar. Outlook shows an editable bar that covers the chosen time (or one time slot, depending on the calendar's time scale) after you let off of the mouse button.
- Type the appointment's identifying name in the editable bar. Outlook generates an appointment with the default availability and reminder time as soon as you start typing.
- The calendar features scaling handles at the top and bottom for editing appointments.
- Drag the top or bottom size lever to adjust the appointment time frame.

- To create the appointment, click away from the bar or press Enter.

TO PLAN AN OCCASION

- Launch a fresh window for appointments.
- Type the event's distinguishing name in the Subject box.
- If applicable, enter the event location in the Location box. You can also include any other information you would like to have in the event header.
- Type or choose the event date in the Start time field. Next, check the box for "All day event" at the right end of the row.
- Type in any extra details, just like you would for an appointment. After that, save and end the event.

Or

- Bring up the calendar's Calendar view.

Take one of the actions listed below:

- On the day you wish to create the event, click the area beneath the day and date and above the time slots in the Day, Work Week, or Week arrangement of the calendar. This is the time slot for the event.
- Click the day you wish to create the event in the calendar's Month arrangement.
- Type in the event's title and hit Enter.

CHAPTER FIVE

CONVERT CALENDAR ITEMS

Every Outlook calendar item is constructed using the same fundamental structure. A calendar item is defined as an appointment, event, or meeting by these two factors:

- Whether the item is available all day or has set start and end hours.
- Whether you use Outlook to invite others.

Converting an appointment into a meeting or event, or an event into an appointment or an invited event, is a simple process. By dragging the email message to the calendar, you may quickly set up a meeting, event, or appointment based on the details in the message. For instance, you can put information about a local art gallery's grand opening on your calendar if a friend or coworker sends you a message with the specifics. To ensure that you (or other meeting participants) have the information available when you need it, you can save any or all of the message content as a calendar item. You can remove the actual message from your inbox once the calendar item has been created.

USING AN EMAIL TO SET UP AN APPOINTMENT

- Make your inbox visible.

- Drag the message to the Calendar button or link on the Navigation Bar from the message list.

- To establish an appointment based on the message and open the appointment window for editing, let go of the mouse button once the cursor turns to a plus sign. The original message's subject and content are included in the appointment. The current time is followed by the next half-hour increment for the start and end times.

Decide on the appointment's date and time, then take one of the following actions:

- Modify the availability, reminder time, or repetition in the Options group.

- Change the appointment's priority, label it as private, or give it a category in the Tags group.

- Modify the original message's content in the content window to meet the appointment's needs.

- To save the appointment to your calendar, click the Save & Close button in the appointment window.

TO TURN A SCHEDULED MEETING INTO AN EVENT

- Launch the window for appointments.

- Choose the All day event check box located at the right end of the Start time row.
- Modify the event window's date, settings, or tags, then save and exit.

MAKING A MEETING OUT OF AN APPOINTMENT

- Launch the window for appointments.
- To add a To box to the header and show the meeting window features, click the Invite Attendees button on the Appointment tab in the Attendees group.
- Type in the contact details of the individuals you wish to invite to the meeting.
- Click the Send Invitation button after adding a location if needed.

TO CHANGE A GATHERING INTO ONE THAT IS INVITED

- The event window should open.
- To add a To box to the header and show the meeting window features, click the Invite Attendees button in the Attendees group on the Event tab.
- Type in the contact details of the individuals you like to invite to the gathering.
- Click the Send Invitation button after adding a location if needed.

MAKING AN APPOINTMENT OUT OF AN EVENT

- The event window should open.
- Select the All day event check box located at the right end of the Start time row.
- Establish the start and end times of the appointment and make any required adjustments. After that, save the appointment window and close it.

SET UP THE CALENDAR ITEM SETTINGS

Meetings, events, and appointments all have a lot in common, and you work with those options in all kinds of calendar entries using the same methods. You can set up the following options for every item:

- Time zones
- A reminder Outlook
- Recurrence
- Privacy

TIME ZONES

The time zone in which a meeting, event, or appointment takes place can be specified. When you're traveling or inviting individuals from different time zones to an online conference, this helps to make sure that the start and end hours are well-defined. It is possible to designate distinct time zones for the start and finish times. This is helpful if you want your "appointment" to appear correctly wherever you are right now and your "appointment" is an aircraft flight with departure and arrival cities in different time zones. Availability When you create an appointment or event, you designate it as Free, Working Elsewhere, Tentative, Busy, or Out Of Office to indicate your availability (also known as Free/Busy time). On your calendar, the appointment or event is color-coded according to your specified availability. When you share your calendar or communicate calendar information to others, your availability is seen to other Outlook users on your network. For events, the default availability is Free; for new appointments and meetings, it is Busy.

A REMINDER OUTLOOK

A reminder Outlook automatically shows a reminder message 12 hours before to an event (at noon on the day before) or 15 minutes before the start of an appointment or meeting. If you would like, you can disable the reminder entirely or set it to go off up to two weeks in advance. Reminders will show up on your mobile device if you sync your Outlook installation with it. When you are not near your computer, this is really handy.

RECURRENCE

You can create a recurring item in your Outlook calendar if you have the same appointment, event, or meeting on a regular basis, such as a weekly fitness class, a monthly team meeting, or an anniversary. Almost any regular interval, like every Tuesday and Thursday, every other week, or the final weekday of every month, can be used to schedule a recurring calendar event.

Setting up a recurrence makes the item on your calendar appear more than once at the time interval you designate. The item can be configured to end after a specific number of repetitions, to end by a specific date, or to repeat until further notice. The repeating item's individual instances are connected. When creating

If a recurring item changes, you have the option to update each instance or only a specific appointment instance. On the calendar, recurrent items are denoted by circling arrows.

PRIVACY

If you want to make sure that the information isn't visible when you share your calendar or transmit calendar information to others, you can mark an item as private. On the calendar, private items are denoted by a lock and are not identified by the subject but rather as Private Appointment to others.

When creating an item, you can identify it as private and include information about **time zones**, your **availability**, the **reminder time**, and the **recurrence**. As an alternative, you can configure any of these parameters when you edit the item later. Only the item window allows you to alter the time zone; the other settings can be adjusted on the item type-specific tool tab that shows on the Outlook ribbon when you choose an item on the calendar, or on the item type-specific tab in the item window. These tabs are called Appointment, Event, Meeting, or Invited Event in single-occurrence items. Occurrence or Series are included in the tab titles of recurring items to indicate whether you are modifying one or all of the item's occurrences.

As with messages and other Outlook objects, appointments, events, and meetings can be categorized and given priority. In some respects, the Calendar's categories are more helpful than those in other modules.

TO INDICATE THE TIME ZONE FOR A MEETING OR APPOINTMENT

- The item window should open.

- To see the time zone controls in the Start Time and End Time rows, select the Time Zones button in the Options group on the Appointment or Meeting tab. The time zone that your computer is now in is shown by the time zone controls.

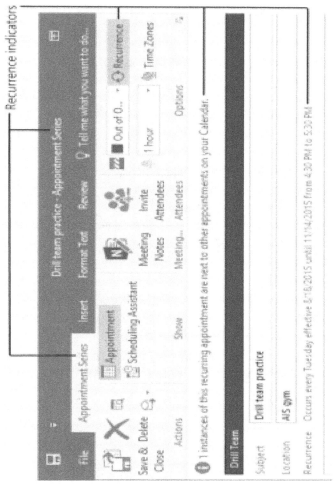

- Click the time zone after selecting the control you wish to modify.

To guarantee that the time is correct from wherever, set the time zones.

TO CONCEAL THE TIME ZONE SETTINGS

- In the "Start time" and "End time" time zone controls, choose the same entries.
- To remove the controls, select the Time Zones button in the Options group on the Appointment or Meeting tab.

TO CHANGE A MEETING, EVENT, OR APPOINTMENT

- Show the calendar with the appointment visible in the Day, Work Week, or Week arrangement of the Calendar view.
- To pick an item in the calendar pane, click on it once.

Next, take one of the following actions:

- Modify the settings or tags on the tool tab according to the item type.
- To modify the start time of an appointment, drag the top sizing handle.

- Drag the item from the current time slot to a new time slot.
- To modify the end time of an appointment, drag the bottom sizing lever.

One of the following actions will open the item window, where you can make more changes:

- Press Enter.
- Click Open in the Actions group on the tool tab corresponding to the item type.

TO SHOW THAT YOU ARE AVAILABLE FOR A MEETING, EVENT, OR APPOINTMENT

- Either choose the item on the calendar or open the item window.
- Select the Show As list in the Options group on the item-specific or tool tab, and then select the availability.

TO MODIFY AN APPOINTMENT, EVENT, OR MEETING'S DEFAULT REMINDER

- Either choose the item on the calendar or open the item window.

- Select the Reminder list in the Options group on the item-specific or tool tab, and then select the time (or

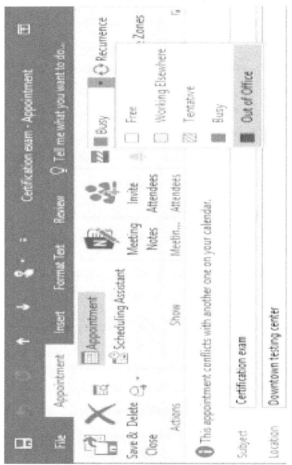

None to have no reminder).

CHAPTER SIX

TO ESTABLISH RECURRING APPOINTMENTS, EVENTS, OR MEETINGS

- Either choose the item on the calendar or open the item window.

- To enter the Recurrence dialog box, select the Recurrence button in the Options group on the item-specific or tool tab. Weekly on the day of the week that is now selected is the default recurrence.

- The Appointment Recurrence dialog box allows you to modify the times, days, and frequency of a recurrence.

Take one of the following actions in the Recurrence dialog box:

- Choose an end time for the recurring meeting by clicking the arrow in the End list.

- Choose the frequency of the meeting's recurrence in the Recurrence pattern box.

- Choose the number of times you would like the meeting to happen or the last date you would like it to happen in the Range of Recurrence area.

- To update the Start Time and End Time boxes in the appointment window with the recurrence information, click OK in the Recurrence dialog box.

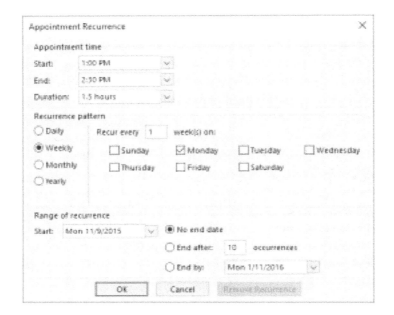

SET UP AND MODIFY MEETINGS

Finding a time that works for everyone who has to attend is a major challenge when setting up a meeting. Compared to alternative ways, Outlook makes meeting scheduling much easier, especially when you need to take into account multiple people's calendars. Outlook shows the individual and group schedules of those who work for your company as well as those of persons from other companies whose calendars have been made public online. You can use Outlook to select a time that works for you, or you can look at the schedules of the attendees to find a time when everyone is available.

Anybody with an email address, including those who don't use Outlook, can get an Outlook meeting invitation (also known as a meeting request). Any kind of email account, including Internet or Exchange accounts, can be used to make a meeting request.

The Appointment page and the Scheduling Assistant page are the two pages that make up the meeting window. By default, the Appointment page is displayed. You can utilize the Scheduling Assistant page's extra capabilities to determine the ideal time for the meeting, or you can enter all the necessary information directly on the Appointment page.

THE MEETING WINDOW'S APPOINTMENT PAGE

On the right side of every meeting window page, the Room Finder is automatically open. This useful tool assists you in determining the best times and days for the greatest number of attendees as well as the locations that are available. The group's overall availability for each day is shown in the monthly calendar located at the top of the Room Finder as follows:

- Nonworking days and dates that fall outside of the workday are not available (gray).
- Good (white) days are those on which every attendee is available.
- Fair (light blue) days have the highest attendance.
- Poor (medium blue) days are those when the majority of attendees are unavailable.

The Room Finder's center displays managed conference rooms that are available at the specified meeting time. Attendee availability for appointments lasting the nine hours you have designated for the meeting is shown in the Suggested Times list at the bottom of the Room Finder pane. The recommended meeting times for that specific day are displayed when you select a date in the calendar. (Scheduling recommendations for nonworking or previous days are not given.) The calendar and the meeting request are updated when a time is selected from the list of suggested times. Attendees are the people you invite to meetings. Each attendee's presence is automatically marked as required. By designating non-essential guests' attendance as optional, you can let them know about the meeting. You can use a distribution list or contact group to invite whole groups of people. Additionally, you can invite managed resources that have been configured by the Exchange administrator of your company, like conference spaces and audio/visual equipment. A meeting request needs to have a start time and an end time, and at least one person other than you should be

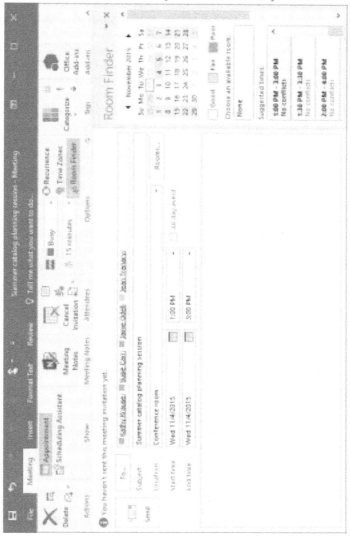

present. A subject and a location should also be included, but if you specifically permit Outlook to do so, it will send the meeting request without these details. A meeting request's body may contain text, links to websites, and attachments. This is a practical method of providing attendees with meeting information in advance.

If your email account is connected to an Exchange Server network, the Scheduling Assistant page is the meeting window's secondary page. If not, the Scheduling page—which is devoid of the Room Finder feature—is the secondary page.

You can check group schedule information on the Scheduling or Scheduling Assistant page if you're planning a meeting for a lot of people. A group schedule that displays each attendee's time status throughout your working day is available on the Scheduling and Scheduling Assistant pages. Outlook shows the time of your proposed meeting on the group calendar. The typical free/busy colors and patterns that correspond to the legend at the bottom of the page show whether or not meeting attendees can access free/busy information. Outlook displays the time with gray diagonal stripes if no information is available (either because it is unable to connect to an attendee's calendar or because the proposed meeting is farther away than the server-stored scheduling information). The combined schedule of all attendees is shown in the row at the top of the schedule, to the right of the All Attendees heading.

By choosing a new time in the Start Time and End Time lists, dragging the vertical start and end time bars in the group schedule, or clicking the desired time in the Suggested Times list, you can modify the meeting's timing and duration to accommodate the schedules that are shown. Outlook provides you with an up-to-date report on the number of attendees at your meeting by tracking answers from attendees and those in charge of arranging the resources you asked. When you open a meeting in its own window, the meeting header section shows the number of people who have accepted, tentatively accepted, and denied the meeting invitation. After sending out the meeting request, you may need to add or delete attendees or alter the meeting's date, time, or location. Any information in a meeting request can be changed at any time by the meeting organizer, including the addition or deletion of participants or the cancellation of the meeting. Updates are given to meeting participants. To enable attendees to easily identify any changes to the meeting arrangements, they are monitored.

TO LAUNCH A FRESH WINDOW FOR MEETINGS

Take one of the following actions:

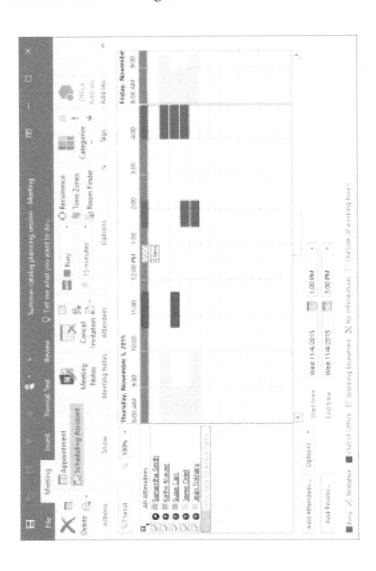

- Click New Meeting under the New group on the Calendar module's Home tab.

- Click New Items in the New group on the Home tab of any module, and then click Meeting. Ctrl+Shift+Q can be pressed in any module.

TO INITIATE A REQUEST FOR A MEETING

- Launch a fresh window for the meeting.

- Type the attendees' contact details in the To box.

- Type the meeting's identifying name in the Subject field.

- Type the meeting place in the Location box. If Skype for Business is used by your company, you can enter Skype meeting details in the Location box and content pane by clicking the Skype Meeting icon on the Meeting toolbar.

- Enter or choose a date and time in the Start time row. A half hour after the start time, Outlook automatically sets the End Time.

- Enter or choose a date and time in the End time row. A meeting may take place over several days or even overnight.

- Check the meeting information, then click Send to add the meeting to your calendar and send the attendees a meeting request.

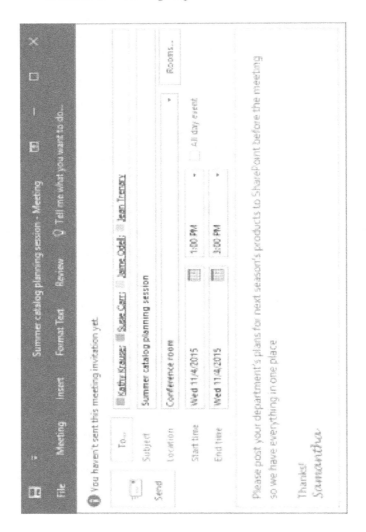

TO FIND OUT WHEN COWORKERS ARE AVAILABLE FOR MEETINGS

- Select the Scheduling Assistant button under the Show group on the Meeting tab. You and any attendees you put in the To box are listed in the Scheduling Assistant page's All Attendees list. You are the meeting organizer, as indicated by the magnifying glass icon in a black circle next to your name. An upward-pointing arrow in a red circle next to each attendee's name indicates that they are expected to be there.

- To see the list of suggested times, if required, scroll to the bottom of the Room Finder. The timings displayed are determined by your schedule as well as the participants' accessible schedule information.

- Press Tab to update the Suggested Times list in the Room Finder after adding attendees by entering their email addresses in the All Attendees list.

- The start and end time bars on the group schedule can be dragged, or times can be entered in the boxes below the group schedule, if you need to modify the meeting's time or length.

- To get back to the Appointment page, which displays the current attendees and meeting hours, click the Appointment button in the Show group.

- After making sure the meeting information is correct, click Send to add the meeting to your calendar and send the attendees a meeting request.

CHAPTER SEVEN
TO MAKE CHANGES TO A MEETING REQUEST

To edit, open the meeting window.

- Outlook asks you to pick whether you wish to change the entire series of meetings or just the chosen instance if the meeting is part of a series (a recurring meeting). Click the full series or just this one.

- Change the attendees, options, notes, date, and time. Next, press the "Send Update" button.

- Outlook asks you to choose whether to send updates to everyone or just the attendees you altered if you made changes to the attendees. To send meeting updates, click one of the following links: Send updates to all attendees or only those who have been added or removed.

TO CALL OFF A MEETING OR AN EVENT THAT INVOLVES MEETINGS

Either open the meeting window or pick the meeting from your calendar. Take one of the actions listed below:

- Click the Cancel Meeting button in the Actions group on the Meeting tool tab.

- Select Cancel Meeting from the Actions group on the Meeting Series tool tab, followed by Cancel

Occurrence or Cancel Series. A meeting window with cancellation details appears.

Take one of the actions listed below:

- Click the Send Cancellation button in the meeting header. Outlook deletes the meeting from the participants' calendars and sends them an updated meeting request.

- Click the Close button (X) at the right end of the message window title bar if you decide to call off the meeting. Outlook gives you options and reminds you that you haven't sent the cancelation. Click Don't cancel the meeting and close in the resulting dialog box, and then click OK. A meeting cannot be canceled without informing the participants.

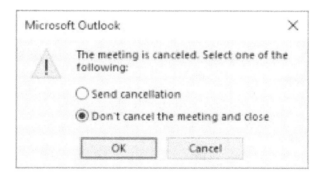

ATTEND TO REQUESTS FOR MEETINGS

When another Outlook user sends you a meeting request, the meeting shows up on your calendar with your time marked as tentative. The organizer is unsure of your attendance until you reply to the meeting request.

A REQUEST FOR A MEETING IN THE READING PANE

You are aware of any scheduling problems at the time of the meeting because the meeting request shows your current calendar information. There are four ways you can reply to a request for a meeting:

- Give in to the request. Outlook adds the meeting to your calendar and removes the meeting request. Accept the request tentatively. This choice shows that you are unsure but may be able to make it to the meeting. Outlook marks the meeting as tentatively booked on your calendar and removes the meeting request.

- Suggest a different time for the meeting. Outlook displays the appointment with the original time on your calendar as provisionally planned and forwards your request to the meeting organizer for confirmation.

- Reject the request. Outlook removes the meeting from your calendar and deletes the meeting request.

The meeting is still listed on your calendar with your time marked as provisionally planned and the meeting details in gray type instead of black if you don't reply to a meeting request.

- You have the option to respond to the meeting organizer when you accept or decline a meeting. The organizer won't know whether you intend to attend the meeting if you don't respond, and your acceptance won't be recorded. If you reply, you can include a note for the meeting host before sending it.

TO REPLY TO A REQUEST FOR A MEETING

- Select Accept, Tentative, or Decline from the shortcut menu that shows up when you right-click the meeting request, the meeting window, or the Reading Pane.

- Decide if you want to send a generic response, a customized response, or nothing at all.

TO SUGGEST A NEW MEETING TIME

To access the Propose New Time dialog box, first click Propose New Time in the meeting window or Reading Pane.

Next, select Tentative and Propose New Time or Decline and Propose New Time from the options.

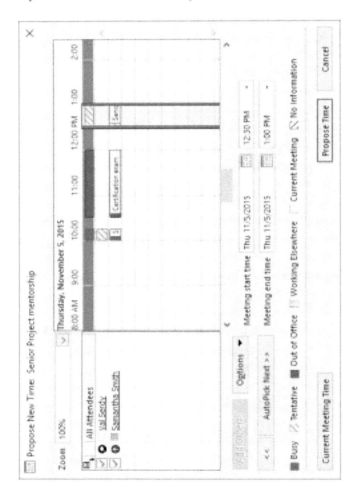

- Click the Propose Time button after modifying the start and end times of the meeting in the Propose

New Time dialog box. You may do this by sliding the start and end time bars or by modifying the date and time in the lists.

- Click Send to add the meeting to your calendar as tentatively planned for the original meeting time. If you would like to send a message to the meeting organizer, do so in the meeting response window that opens. You and the other attendees will receive revised meeting requests with the new time if the meeting organizer authorizes the change.

PRESENT SEVERAL CALENDARS VIEWS.

You have the same control over how Outlook presents calendar data (the view) and how that data is organized (the arrangement) as you have with other Outlook modules.

There are four content views in the Calendar module:

- **Calendar**: This is how your Outlook calendar is typically shown. In the Calendar view of the Day, Work Week, or Week arrangement, each appointment, meeting, or event's subject, location, and organizer (if available) are shown alongside the availability bar and any unique icons, like Private or Recurrence.

- **A sneak peek:** As space permits, more information, including data from the appointment window's notes section, is displayed in the Preview view for the Day, Work Week, or Week arrangement.
- **List:** This list view shows all of your calendar's events, meetings, and appointments.
- **Active:** Only upcoming appointments, meetings, and events are shown in this list view.

You can organize calendar entries in a list view by choosing a field from the View tab's Arrangement gallery. Depending on the view, many layouts are available. The following are among the time-span-based arrangements in Calendar view and Preview view:

- One day at a time, divided into half-hour intervals, is displayed.
- Work Week: Only the days of your work week are displayed. Monday through Friday, from 8:00 a.m. to 5:00 p.m., is the standard workweek. On the calendar, time slots outside of the work week are colored, while those that fall within the work week are white.
- One calendar week (Sunday through Saturday) is displayed at a time.

- One calendar month is shown at a time, along with any days that come before or after that correspond to the weeks that are shown.

View of the schedule shows the calendar for the chosen time period in a horizontal perspective.

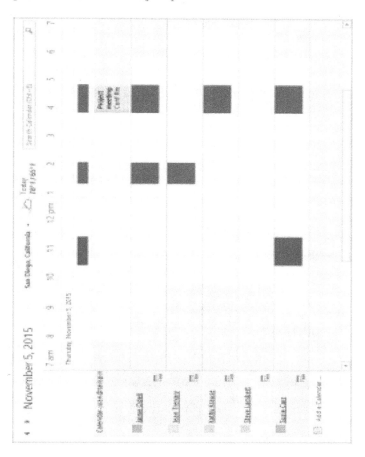

To make it simple to compare several calendars for particular time periods, you can add other people's calendars as rows in this view. Comparing constrained time periods for several calendars, like those of members of a calendar group, is made much easier using this setup. To navigate between arrangements, click the buttons in the Arrangement group on the Calendar module ribbon's View tab. This view allows you to see your full workweek at once.

You can modify the time frame displayed in the calendar by using these extra tools:

- To view the previous or subsequent time period, click the Back or Forward buttons next to the date or range of dates in the calendar header.
- Click the Today button in the Go To group on the Home tab to see the current day. In the Go To group on the Home tab, click the Next 7 Days button to see a seven-day period beginning with the current day.
- Show the week numbers in the Date Navigator and Month view to the left of each week. By putting this choice into practice, you can click the week tab to see that week.

To show a month's worth of your calendar, do one of the following:

- To view your calendar for the month, click the Month button in the Arrange group on the Home tab.
- Hit Ctrl+Alt+4.

To navigate in Month view, use one of the actions listed below:

- Click the Forward or Back buttons to advance or regress the calendar by one month, respectively, to the left of the date range in the calendar header.
- To see more information on the monthly calendar, click the Change View button in the Current View group on the View tab. Then, select Preview in the gallery.

Make use of the Date Navigator

The current and upcoming months are automatically shown in the Date Navigator at the top of the Folder Pane when using the Outlook Calendar module. The current date, the time period shown in the content window, the days you are free, and the days you are busy are all quickly indicated by these small monthly calendars.

One practical and helpful tool is the Date Navigator. A blue square represents the current date. Light blue highlighting indicates the day or dates that are currently shown in the calendar. Days having appointments, meetings, or events planned are shown by bolded dates. The two default calendars display the days of the previous and subsequent months in gray. By adjusting the width or height of the area designated for the Date Navigator, you can show more or fewer months.

Either of the following actions will alter the Date Navigator area's size:

- To make the Folder Pane wider, drag its right edge to the right; to make it wider, drag it to the left.
- To make the Date Navigator calendars taller, drag the horizontal border beneath them up or down.
- Each month is displayed in seven-day weeks in the Date Navigator. The First Day Of Week setting on the Calendar page of the Outlook Options dialog box controls which day of the week appears in the Date Navigator. When more than one month is displayed in the Date Navigator, each month is shown in either five or six weeks, depending on how many days are needed to represent the currently selected month.

Using the Date Navigator, you may choose which day, week, month, or range of days to display on the calendar. When you select a day in the Week arrangement, the calendar's corresponding week is displayed. If not, the calendar arrangement adjusts to display the time frame you choose.

To work with the Date Navigator, employ these strategies:

- Click the date to see that day. Point to the left edge of the week to display it, then click to choose it when the cursor direction shifts from left to right. Week numbers can be shown in the Date Navigator and Calendar by configuring the Calendar Options. If you do, the week is displayed when you click on the week number.) Point on the earliest date you wish to display, then drag the Date Navigator to the last date to show a range of days (from two days to a maximum of six weeks).

- Click the Previous or Next arrows at the top of the Date Navigator, on either side of the month name, to modify the time period shown in the calendar one month at a time.

- Press the month name, then drag up or down on the resulting list to go several months forward or backward.

TO MAKE THE CALENDAR SHOW A SEVEN-DAY WEEK

- Point to the left edge of a calendar row with one or more bold dates in the Date Navigator located at the top of the Folder Pane.
- To see the chosen seven-day week in the calendar, click once when the cursor shifts to face the calendar.

Complete one of the following actions to see your work week schedule:

- Click the Work Week button in the Arrange group on the Home tab.
- Press Ctrl+Alt+2.

The top of the window displays the first time slot of your designated workday. Time slots outside of your workday are shaded, while those inside your workday are white. To show your calendar for a single day, click the Day button in the Arrangement group on the View tab. This will only show the schedule for the day you have chosen.

TO SHOW THE SCHEDULE FOR TODAY

- Click the Today button in the Go To group on the Home tab. The current week is now displayed on the calendar if it wasn't already. The times that are shown don't change. The highlighted times reflect the current day and time slot.
- Click the Daily Task List button in the Layout group on the View tab.

Take one of the following actions to have your task list appear on the Calendar:

- To see the work list section beneath the calendar, click Normal.
- To see a single row beneath the calendar, click Minimized. The number of your daily tasks that are active, finished, and total is shown in the reduced Daily Task List.
- To conceal the task list, click Off.

TO RESTORE THE CALENDAR'S ORIGINAL CONFIGURATION

- To restore the calendar to its original configuration, select Calendar from the Change View gallery.
- To restore the default calendar state, select Reset View in the Current View group.

CHAPTER EIGHT

REVIEW OF SKILLS

These chapters taught you how to:

- Plan events and appointments:
- Convert calendar items
- Set up calendar item preferences
- Arrange and modify meetings
- Attend to meeting requests
- Present various calendar views

MAKE PLANS FOR EVENTS AND APPOINTMENTS

Launch Outlook, then see your calendar. Next, do the following:

- Make a new appointment and set it up as follows for the SBS Study Session: Decide on a date that is one week from now. The timing should be set between 11:30 a.m. and 12:30 p.m.
- Indicate the Library Meeting Room as the location.
- Save and end the appointment while maintaining all other default settings.
- Establish National Dessert Day as a new all-day event and set it up as follows:

- Change the date to October 14, the next occurrence. Save and end the event while maintaining all other default settings.

CONVERT CALENDAR ITEMS

After displaying your inbox, take the following actions:

- Find the message you sent yourself during the SBS Test, "Send and receive email messages."

Based on the communication, make an appointment and set it up as follows:

- SBS Rafting Trip should be the new subject instead of SBS Test.
- Decide on Saturday of next week and set the time between 11:00 a.m. and 2:00 p.m.
- Indicate "To Be Determined" as the location.
- Save and end the appointment while maintaining all other default settings.
- Make your calendar visible.

After finding the appointment for the SBS Rafting Trip, take the following actions:

- Make the appointment an all-day event. Save and end the event while maintaining all other default settings.

Find the SBS Rafting Trip event, then take the subsequent actions:

- Bring a friend along to the event.
- I'm honing my Outlook scheduling skills in the content pane. Kindly accept this invitation.
- Forward the invitation to the event.

SET UP THE CALENDAR ITEM SETTINGS

After displaying your calendar, take the following actions:

- Find the appointment for the SBS Study Session that you made in the first practice exercise for this chapter.
- Show the time zone controls when the appointment window opens.
- Set the start and end times to take place in a time zone one hour ahead of your own.
- Select "Out of Office" for your availability during the appointment.
- One hour prior to the appointment, set a reminder.
- Set up the appointment to repeat every month on the first Monday and to terminate after three occurrences.
- Close and save the series of appointments.

SET UP AND MODIFY MEETINGS

This exercise is intended for Outlook users working in Exchange settings. After displaying your calendar, take the following actions:

Create a new meeting with the subject SBS Project Review, and set it as follows:

- Invite a colleague from your Exchange network. Choose My Office as the location. Decide on next Thursday as the date.
- To find out about availability, select the Date Navigator in the Room Finder and scroll through the list of suggested times. Select a half-hour time window that displays "No conflicts" from the list of suggested hours.

Open the meeting invitation's Scheduling Assistant page and take the following actions:

- Await the presentation of your colleague's availability on the group calendar. Take note of the color blocks that show each person's and the group's availability and working hours. Make that the time you have chosen is displayed as being open for both of you. If not, drag the start and finish time markers to adjust the time.

- Go back to the meeting invitation's Appointment page and confirm the details. Enter "I'm practicing scheduling meetings" in the content pane. Kindly agree to this meeting request. Next, send out the invitation to the meeting.
- Find the SBS Project Review meeting on your calendar and click the meeting window.

Open the meeting window's Scheduling Assistant page, then take the following actions:

- Add a colleague to the list of attendees and watch for their availability to appear on the group calendar.
- To find out when you and your coworkers are busy or not in the office, go back and forth a few days on the group calendar.
- If required, modify the time and date of the meeting by choosing them from the section beneath the group calendar.
- Go back to the meeting invitation's Appointment page and confirm the details. The meeting update should then be sent to everyone present.

ATTEND TO REQUESTS FOR MEETINGS

This exercise is intended for Outlook users working in Exchange settings. After displaying your inbox, take the following actions:

- Request a meeting request from a coworker.
- After receiving the meeting request, open it after reviewing the contents in the Reading Pane.
- Open your calendar from the meeting request window. Take note of the hues and designs that stand for the rejected meeting request and your availability at that moment.
- Go back to the request for the meeting. Give a tentative response and suggest a different time for the meeting.

PRESENT SEVERAL CALENDARS VIEWS

After displaying your calendar in calendar view, take the following actions:

- Show your current month's calendar.
- Take note of the shading that indicates the current day in the Date Navigator.
- To view your calendar for only that day, click on another day that has no appointments. The day of your next appointment will then appear on your

calendar when you click the Next Appointment bar on the right side of the day.

- Select the Work Week calendar layout and enable the Daily Task List to appear beneath the calendar.

- To see just your upcoming appointments, events, and meetings, switch to your calendar's Active view.

- You can update the calendar to include the holidays in your nation or area if you'd like. Observe how the calendar material in the Active view has changed.

- Customize the Calendar to provide the view and layout that you choose.

CONCLUSION

In this tutorial book, we've explored the essential features and functionalities of Microsoft Outlook, equipping you with the knowledge to manage your emails, calendars, and tasks effectively. From setting up your account to mastering advanced tools, you've learned how to enhance your productivity and streamline your communication.

Outlook is not just an email client; it's a comprehensive tool for organizing your professional and personal life. By utilizing its features—such as calendar sharing, task management, and integration with other Microsoft applications—you can improve your workflow and ensure that nothing falls through the cracks.

As you continue to use Outlook, remember to explore its updates and new features, as Microsoft frequently enhances the application. Stay curious and keep experimenting with its capabilities to find new ways to simplify your tasks.

Thank you for joining us on this journey through Microsoft Outlook. We hope this book has provided you with the insights and skills needed to make the most of this powerful tool. Happy emailing!